# The Heart of It

# The Heart of It

Poems by

Alan Perry

© 2025 Alan Perry. All rights reserved.
This material may not be reproduced in any form, published,
reprinted, recorded, performed, broadcast,
rewritten, or redistributed without
the explicit permission of Alan Perry.
All such actions are strictly prohibited by law.

Cover design by Shay Culligan
Cover image by Skyler Ewing on Unsplash
Author photo by Kim Pufahl

ISBN: 978-1-63980-748-2

Kelsay Books
502 South 1040 East, A-119
American Fork, Utah 84003
Kelsaybooks.com

*to Kris*
*for all the poems yet to write*

# Acknowledgments

I am very grateful to the editors of the publications in which these poems first appeared, sometimes in earlier versions or different forms:

*Broadkill Review:* "Descent," "Traveling Water"
*Eclectica Magazine:* "Mirroring"
*Gyroscope Review:* "Side Door"
*Heron Tree:* "Exoplanet"
*MockingHeart Review:* "Out of Service"
*Ocotillo Review:* "Flying Lesson" as "Flying Lessons"
*Olit:* "Svelte"
*ONE ART:* "At the Barcelona Airport" as "Baggage," "Necessary Matter," "Pulling Over"
*Panoply:* "Coming About"
*Remington Review:* "Dead Letter" as "Flying Lessons"
*San Pedro River Review:* "Flares"
*Sandcutters:* "Voyager"
*Schuylkill Valley Journal:* "Cycles," "Encroachment"
*Stone Circle Review:* "Autumn Redux"
*Stone Poetry Quarterly:* "Tapestry"
*Valparaiso Poetry Review:* "Dear Despair" as "Baggage"

Special thanks to poet, editor, and educator Juliet Patterson for her mentorship over the years. Without her encouragement, guidance, and editing, many of the poems in this book would not have been created.

# Contents

## I.

| | |
|---|---|
| Necessary Matter | 13 |
| Flares | 14 |
| Exoplanet | 16 |
| Voyager | 17 |
| Flying Lessons | 18 |
| Cycles | 20 |
| Autumn Redux | 21 |
| Joy | 22 |
| Observatory | 23 |
| Pulling Over | 24 |
| Recession | 26 |
| Intentions | 27 |
| Encroachment | 28 |
| Some Call It a Sign | 29 |

## II.

| | |
|---|---|
| Grafting | 33 |
| Traveling Water | 35 |
| Descent | 37 |
| Baggage | 38 |
| Coming About | 41 |
| Nick | 42 |
| Svelte | 44 |
| Out of Service | 45 |
| At the Cemetery | 47 |
| Topography Relief | 48 |
| What Uncovers Us | 49 |
| Tapestry | 51 |
| Side Door | 52 |
| Mirroring | 54 |

I.

# Necessary Matter

No matter how a freakish snowfall
burdens the mesquite tree leaning
so heavily it bows to the equinox.

No matter that the median's palo verde
can't bear the weight of change,
halves itself so one shaft survives.

No matter that mourning doves tell me
they are contented with rainfall,
with each other, with their calling.

What matters is the moment
before absence, when recollection swells
amid breakdown, when there's nothing

beyond horizon but sky. That's when
there is no loss, only precedent
for grief—unbounded, sacred.

I want to tell you when my best friend died,
I wasn't there. My phone rang off-key,
rattled and clicked like slipping breath.

There were only liminal spaces before
that winter, half of us bending toward earth
like a snow-laden trunk.

And in the moments after snow melts,
rivers come alive, reservoirs re-fill,
depth gradually returns.

# Flares

Before I began watching stars
I looked for you in every light

that mirrored sunshine.
I thought I saw you in fireworks

sending me messages in bottle rockets
sparkling in front of a moon

with a hidden dark side.
I imagined your face in starbursts

detonating above me until
the aura flamed out

and nothing came of it
but ash and smoky cinders.

Still, I'm enamored with sparks,
eruptions, sonic booms

and the reflexive squint I offer
these earth-bound moonshots.

Though some seem like empty glares
emitted from glowing spheres,

as in the moment a flash bulb
explodes from its camera,

excited by the coming photo.
Only then the light stays

in my eyes imprinted, signaling
I may be starstruck.

# Exoplanet

*Astronomers discover a new star: Trappist-1
and its seven planets—b through h*


I'm relieved to know there's hope for me,
that a Goldilocks character might inhabit

another world. Some water is likely there,
not frozen but free to slide down mountains

and glimmer off the starset, life as I
would want it—warm enough to be nurtured,

strong enough to survive meteor rain, asteroids—
while I wait for the right eon

to be invited to live there and to love
a body called d, e or f—it's hard to see on Earth,

40 light years away from Aquarius.
But I'm patient.

I'll flip through the planets,
focus the telescope and hold my breath

for the fly-by of your light
to reach me.

# Voyager

I found you on a moon of Mars
following trails of frozen canals
distant from a sea of tranquility.
Propelled into solar storms
through a cloudy telescope, I calculated
orbits of when we'd meet, wondering
if this trip was too far to return.

Your red glow flared on the horizon
but a core attraction held me—
a thaw in your icy landscape.
I scanned for an earthrise
above your mountainous shoulders
as you paused, rotating until
all I saw was shadow.

Alone like an exoplanet,
I want to know if you will stay
on this rock in deep space,
breathe its thin atmosphere
with me, find the next sign of life.
Or will you leave the ash of us—
stone and dust of what's come before—
and search for another distant satellite
invisible to the naked eye
but always moving, circling?

## Flying Lessons

       i.

We kissed a long goodbye in the hotel lobby
as the cab curled into the driveway.

Athens stoplights blinked their farewells
in the 3:00 am darkness, speeding me

to the airport. You will fly the same plane,
same flight, same seat in a week

after your Greek party cruise with girlfriends.
In seat 26D I scribbled lavish lines

to you, tucked the poem under my cushion
above the life vest. I was certain no one cleans

a 777 well enough to pull and toss hidden notes.
My email told you where to find the message

that began with *I love.* Your email
reply began with *I can't*—


       ii.

Your eyeglass case will sit
adjacent to your right hand

while you write in arcing cursive.
A half-empty Perrier nearby,

sleek, ringless fingers
will sweep across lines

as your left hand flattens
the paper, pinning it in place.

Now I want you to speak to me
the way that I did not,

tell me where your heart is
since it has been alone.

With your head bowed, words
will easily shape themselves, express

their ink and intentions toward me—
extensions of the last *goodbye* in Athens,

the unresponsive texts.
I'll anticipate the letter's arrival,

its return address smudged
by hands that held the envelope

before I did. The slitting of a paper seal
the only motion I can predict,

not knowing if the words
to follow *I can't* will be

*take back my leaving.*

## Cycles

The washing machine hisses as it sprays
water over soiled laundry, mixing soap

I poured in the tub—food to fuel its work.
The cylinder surges as fabrics lilt up and down

gently pulsing dirt out of clothes
down the drain, like the way we shed

our epithelia, bits and flakes at a time,
re-inventing skin that protects us.

As the cleansing nears completion,
the machine rumbles, bangs

against the wall, thumps on the floor.
Damp clothes begin their wind down, spinning

in a force that keeps them pressed together.
The sequence ended, I notice sheets

wrap themselves around everything,
like legs tangled in bed, clinging tighter

than skin on skin, silk to satin.
I gently peel apart the cottons and linens,

my pant leg knotted around a blouse—
her bra entwined with my shirt so firmly

they look inseparable. But they're not.
Delicate things need to breathe.

# Autumn Redux

*after Mary Oliver*

Don't you mourn summer's lapse
in fuchsia leaves that scuttle past you?
Don't you feel the brush of hair
as wind dances around you, encircling
your body in fall's pollen?
Naked trees stand firm, skin closing
tightly to repel brutish cold.
You've seen the turn that comes
with early sunsets, remember
what was only temporary shade.
Doesn't it feel like the lover
who leaves you alone, memories piled
at your feet, rake in your hands
trying to collect what's scattering?
There's little you can do except
tie the scarf she made for you
tighter against the loss.
Air fills with flakes,
ground hardens beneath your step
as animals find their shelter.
You know the cycles, recognize
temperatures and barometers of pressure,
understand their liquids when they fall.
You feel the chill of absence,
the empty space of *I'm leaving now.*

# Joy

It's not the dog wagging
its tail at my approach

or the butterfly pausing
in front of my face.

And it doesn't show up
in the warm summer shower

that greens everything it touches.
But it's in the scribbled note

you left me about groceries,
the kids and their homework,

your stressful workday schedule.
And it's especially the way you look

at me as you walk up the driveway
as if to ask for one of those

exquisite moments when every song
includes your favorite chord,

every door seems to open
without effort or ache,

and all I can give you
is the promise *I'm here.*

# Observatory

My wife pulls me to the front door
where a bird perches near the side window.
A vivid sunburst yellow, it jumps
from profile to head-on view

then back, one eye then two,
fascinated by its human gawkers.
*American goldfinch* my wife proclaims,
showing off her birding expertise—*a symbol*

*of unbridled joy, a positive spirit.* I'm amazed
at its golden body, streaked wing and cap
of black, tinged with white touches
as if paint-brushed while it flew past.

It stands peering into our house, seems
to ask what is in here that holds our life.
Canadian fire smoke continues its swim
in our local airstream, tainting atmosphere,

darkening skies by noon.
This will eventually pass, as will
the goldfinch whose brilliance will outlast
those somber shades in the filmy distance.

If I open the door, the bird will flit
from view, find a more suitable home
than ours. But for the moment, we share
the awe of each other's company—

three watchers craving color
that becomes light.

# Pulling Over

The figure emerges in my rearview mirror
shadowed by a dimly lit sunset.

It may be my father, guiding the miles ahead,
my young hands on the wheel, teaching

me to steer into an oncoming turn.
Or showing me how to change oil,

replace worn tires, tune the engine
so all the pieces work together.

But it could be my mother extending
her forearm in front of my chest,

a maternal seatbelt holding me away
from the dashboard, inches from my head.

Most likely, it's you in mirrored glass
waving hello and goodbye, smiling

as I drive our Impala, the one
with fins, wind finding open windows,

you sitting next to me, never wanting an exit.
Your hand caresses my neck

while you proclaim our road as endless.
I hear you again, humming to the radio

like tread on pavement, a white noise
of comfort that lingers as I drive,

decelerating as tires swerve to the shoulder.
Idling there in the moment, I remember

how much I wanted to write this down
before I forgot how far we'd driven.

# Recession

The grass, cut long now
lies matted like shag carpet,

turns pale brown
but without dying. At times

it will push up green tufts
near edges of leaves,

then through snow. Like we
who linger in the season

that came before us,
want it all back despite

sunburn, storms, lakes
that overran, and sun-dried beds

that expose withering
capsized boats, the death

of something so long abandoned,
a missing name forgotten.

Only the lines of rock strata
leach white after life recedes

and we ask *Why weren't
we there to stop it?*

# Intentions

Each day, the elderly widower across the street
opens his garage door, sets down
a window box fan, aims it
toward his driveway that faces mine.
I'm puzzled at his purpose—
such a small fan for a two-car space.

Is he venting smelly vapors
from a cabinet-staining project?
Exhausting sawdust from his workbench?
Or maybe drawing special memories in
from his house? He rustles around
in the garage moving boxes, furniture,
knick-knacks in ways I don't understand,
pausing occasionally to lift a piece,
examine it, then gently place it
on the high shelf he built.

His garage door is closed today,
no movement in his house or yard.
But I notice a hummingbird suspends itself
next to his garage, near where the fan
usually rests, as if waiting for draft and lift.
Along my sidewalk I feel a swirl of air
that carries dried leaves from my yard
hurries them down my driveway,
leads me across the street.

# Encroachment

Yellow cactus flowers strike
a welcoming pose, petals
outstretched to meet
a smoky sun. But gray hems
the pot, darkens the ground
with ash, tiny cinders
like charcoal bits on a beach.

We wanted neighboring mesquite,
spiky blooms for our remote
desert home—far from traffic,
buildings, hydrants. But the air,
now nearly on fire in its own storm,
threatens, overrunning
our makeshift fire-break of dirt.

As I throw our go-bag in the truck,
the sky explodes to glower at us,
enflamed by our departure.
In the sideview mirror,
nothing left but an empty hose
spread near the flower pot—
another snake seeking water.

# Some Call It a Sign

A woolly bear caterpillar squirms
across the aging blacktop

in front of me, unaware
of my toes approaching—

a sole about to pancake his frame
like an earthquaked building

too old for its own safety,
too carelessly maintained.

I wonder if he sees
my shadow, the doom

in his day if no one cares.
But I can step aside,

not even graze the hairs
of his accordion body—

such a delicate creature
instinctively doing the work

to get from here to there,
inching to nearby twigs

where he will morph into a tiger moth.
Not like this ruptured walkway

that will again crack and heave,
push up black crust as it crumbles,

no longer sustaining my steps—
no more forward progress

on easy paths to food or water.
Time left, like an achingly slow crawl,

now measured in minutes.

II.

# Grafting

I make a slight incision
in the bark, unaware of how
to perform this intricate surgery.

I am not an arborist who knows
what will hurt or help.
All I want to do is add rings

to this dying boxelder sapling—
extract new life from a giant oak,
try to whittle a healthy twig

into a v-notch slot. The sapling
with its bandaged arm struggles
to stand erect before I stake

the ground wires. The genetics
probably won't combine—
two different trees that never

grow together. They would need to adjust
their forms, re-make leaves
in unknown patterns, eventually

confusing the forestry experts.
But I'll hope for new growth
with abundant moisture

and mulch, add some old powdered
plant food I found in the garage.
This could be called a marriage—

awkward, somewhat artificial,
officiated by my ignorance.
And when asked, I could say

I'm trying to cultivate roots
that dig for common ground,
branches that breathe in unison.

# Traveling Water

Near Newfoundland's coast
humpbacks breach from water
skybound, spinning in pirouettes

off a fishing boat's bow,
then splat their belly flops
in front of a girl spying them.

Her mouth agape, eyes like huge buttons,
she's as curious as the whales
in their wonderment of each other.

But here I sit, no water in sight
as trees bend to the wishes
of wind that directs their boughs

with branches outstretched, and trunks
that lean in late summer heat.
Nothing will burst from this ground

no giant voles to perform arabesques
on my lawn, or shred grass
in a dance toward autumn.

My granddaughter laughs as she
soars on her backyard swing set,
and I point to cumulus clouds

as they drift east northeast, hoping
they will carry my awe, linger
over a boat in Conception Bay

as a father tells his daughter
to turn this way
look for more signs of water

parting, the next miracle
to emerge.

# Descent

From a drone's view, a watercolor print—
shades of blue lean toward shore

as if nudged by undercurrents.
White foam rides urgent water

folding in from the sea to the land
it wants to own—thicker

then thinner where sand recedes.
And above it all, dots of pinkish hue

soar in loose formation, appearing
translucent to land and shore below—

flamingos drift en masse, wings
expand as legs rudder their course.

A picture forms with pin-like precision
groups birds in ever-changing borders

touches each avian point with the care
of a mother moving her children

closer together, even as they fly
into sunsets of vanishing coral.

# Baggage

i.

She pushes her luggage cart
through the concourse, tissue to her eyes.
I barely notice she's crying until
I roll past her with my carry-on.
Her blouse is wrinkled, hair uncombed
and a long sweater wraps itself
around her waist in a hug—remnants
maybe from the Atlanta red-eye.
As I look over my shoulder
she pauses, leans on her cart heaped
with a satchel and two large bags
and seems to compose herself.
She changes her pace intermittently,
checks her phone, then glances
at the glass ceiling as if dawn
signals relief. I feel better
hoping her despair has eased.
Was it bad news from home?
A break-up with her partner?
The death of a loved one?
I want to intrude, ask several
*none-of-your-business* questions,
text the sad scene to friends I'm meeting
in Madrid—but I won't. Certain grief
moves on wheels, brakes for no reason,
then veers off, carrying its weight
to an unexpected exit. At my gate, I see her
pass by again as I queue up for boarding—
her head still bowed as she turns
a sharp corner near the duty-free shop

and disappears down the escalator.
I want her to be on a flight to Istanbul,
where continents meet in narrow straits,
cross over to each other freely, even if
some cargo is never fully unloaded.

ii.

I pass you in an airport
burdened with your carry-ons,
wheels squeaking a slow-motion cry.

The wet tissue near your eyes,
wrinkled clothes you slept in
tangled from crowded skies.

I mistake you for a cancellation,
a one-off to be rescheduled
to a time and place you'd rather be.

I don't understand your gravity,
the weight, the drag of leaden feelings
that can pull me to the ground.

As I rush toward departure
all I ask is to let me pass.
Let me gather my belonging

within a circle of friends
where no one grieves, weeps
or leaves a home where hope resides.

Let me move through freezing tunnels
to a place that coats my flight
in gentle de-icing, embraces me,

keeps me from falling.

# Coming About

Sailboats bobble in the cove
as wind pushes blue-green water
up over decks, then down
in undulating refrain.
Masts stand erect while rolled sails
grab the base of each pole, hold
what won't be released.
One craft rotates in the breeze,
approaches a nearby skiff
nudging bows as they twirl
like bumper cars on floats.
But wind cleaves them apart
bobbers flatten on storm waves.
A couple steers to windward,
tacks through the jostling flotilla
in a scrambled game of chance
to avoid water wrecks.
Their surface time measured
not in nautical miles
but hand-over-hand tasks,
letting out just enough sheet
to sail away from what
might tip them over.

# Nick

As she slid into our favorite booth
I saw the apostrophe on her cheek—

it looked like wet magenta,
the way it curled away

from her upper lip, as if
a smile was starting, though

it wasn't. She said it was
a scratch from the pineapple

she carelessly bit into
before it was sectioned.

Her forced laugh was familiar,
her hand on mine quickly

changing the subject. But
in our twenty-year friendship

she's been known to lie—
when she says she loves to cook

only his favorite dinners,
that little chip on her front tooth,

the blue mark on her throat.
She says he's getting better,

has been wonderful lately
buying her jewelry and new clothes.

You can only deny so much
with make-up.

## Svelte

My thinness always held weight
in the mouths of others.
The skinny words spoken
by football coaches
and friends alike,
the snapping twigs
of adjectives that kept me
on the sidelines.
Even girlfriend comments
about my clothes—better on
than off. Or those about
my monkey arms
when playing basketball,
the slams against my bones
that broke so easily
under pressure.

But I honed a skill to lean
invisibly behind a birch tree,
slip between steel posts
of schoolyard fencing.
I could slice
through a crowd
who wondered how
a glimpse of light
entered the room
and left no shadow.

# Out of Service

My telephone service provider texted the news
they will no longer offer directory assistance—

effective immediately—which seemed
much too abrupt for a loyal customer like me.

I can't help but wonder if someone
was in the middle of a query

searching for Aunt Marge in Minnesota
to tell her Grandpa Joe passed away

the funeral scheduled for next Friday.
Did the caller hear all ten digits

or just the area code
as service was cut off?

It's a big geography with millions of records
to sort. But we've all asked for help once

finding the right numbers to keep track
of Great Grandma's dementia

hear about Mark's first day of college
or the birth of Andrea's new baby.

Though we sometimes found loved ones
when they seemed lost, or we were

and needed special assistance.
Direction came from a soothing voice

on the other end, like a mother
connecting us to our next kin

taking our hands—one finger at a time—
wrapping them tightly around the receiver

not wanting to let us go, to say goodbye
for the last time.

# At the Cemetery

Bees halo my cap as I clip splayed shoots
while ants scurry across *Beloved Father, Dearest Mother,*
just ahead of the gentle sweep of my brush.

They meet me every year on this lawnscape, build homes
around those who live here as permanent family.
My grandkids roam nearby searching for more kin,

though I tell them these are the only plots we own.
In the outlying field, they find tilted sandstone markers—
a Civil War soldier from Minneapolis killed at sixteen,

a mother and daughter who succumbed to the Spanish flu,
an infant's inscription etched in a foreign language.
Unfazed, they return to help trim overgrown headstones,

conversing with their great-great-grandparents.
They chat about school last week as they snip weeds,
then ask about their lives—*What country were you born in?*

*Where did you live? Did you have kids like me?*
My knees twinge as I get up to survey our work.
A light rain begins and the edger has lost power

so we pack up the tools. As we walk to the car,
my granddaughter points to our remaining blank stone.
She whispers to her brother, *I'll take care of this one.*

# Topography Relief

*after the painting "Western Storms" by Ed Mell*

I'm invited to sit with sharp angles
that cut mountains in ways

only tectonic plates could create. Sheared
at odd slants, cliffs and mesas form

a bladed landscape, lined like a ruler,
colored with a wide palette.

Rain forms like obelisks, drenched
in prism shades, glancing blows

of clean-edged downpours.
Clouds queue up in crystal shapes—

diamond clusters of pantone, trapezoids
in layered orange hues, thunderheads

as mountain-sized boulders. I'm enticed
into a cubist universe, askew

in its contrasts, dark like a coming storm.
But I hesitate to step into this plane

of finely-honed blocks. I need
soft edges of ambiguity, a pentimento

depth to be explored, the geometry
of earth in a curved horizon—

shapeless water, aurora light.

# What Uncovers Us

Lifting snow from one yard to the next,
wind drives this blizzard at sharp angles,

re-channels streets, re-forms buried lawns
into mounds of irregular slopes.

I glance at the window all day to see
if the snowplow service will appear

but his 24-hour guarantee is
apparently, at any minute,

24 hours away. My back tightens,
signals a coming ache as my hands

begin to chill in anticipation
of a no-show plow truck.

Like furnace heat in winter
I stay inside today, protect

a core of hibernation, retreat
from what howls outside.

In the middle of the night, a dream:
rumbling sounds in the cul-de-sac,

engines revving nearby, metal
scraping pavement, then silence

as I imagine snow disappearing
effortlessly in the dark. Dawn

forces me outside with a shovel
to find my driveway cleared,

a bare sidewalk, snow piled
like levees, and I realize this

is what I'll always want more of—
another day to uncover

earth at its edges.

# Tapestry

Gesturing on a cloth map,
she points me where to scrawl next,

her plan for an inky quilt
that builds, square by square,

reveals a patchwork she calls
warp and weft. I call it a poem, she

declares it a wall hanging. I insist
it displays as lines, form,

but she loves it as fabric.
My words jut at right angles,

new images in her loom.
And when I finish writing, she wants

the piece suspended like an intricate rug
that mixes each scrap of language.

But our own picture—tan bodies
on a white beach—decorates the breezeway,

faded from too much sun, gave up
its two ghosts to a colorless background.

Waving me into the art studio,
air sweeps the space she walked—

her feet on bare floor,
walls that spoke in patterns.

## Side Door

Where deliveries arrive
mistakenly or with purpose
the fulfillment of what I need:

water filters for the refrigerator,
organic oatmeal, dog food,
chamomile tea to quiet the noise.

It opens easily to the sounds
of friendly chatter in the doorway,
rehashing the overtime ballgame,

neighbor kids invading the house.
And for casseroles baked
in celebration and in sympathy

along with that long-forgotten
borrowed rake from three years ago.
This door closes so gently with air

compressing its mechanism
as if there should be no slams
no finality of a latch and lock

but simply a screen to welcome
breezes and light, an invitation
to outside beauty. Like the day you

rang the bell, asked for directions
then later coffee, and finally, a chair.
Your hand on the doorknob wanting

no formality or RSVP through the mail.
Just you with the freshness
of outdoor freedom and your smile

opening like a sunflower
as you stepped through
the only entrance without a key,

and stayed.

# Mirroring

I imagine you found me beyond your frame
bustling around in our closet, sorting clothes—
scarves that needed hanging,
a wedding dress to be boxed, sweaters
that warmed the coldest ocean chill.
I didn't see you in the luminescence
or bright reflection of daylight,
not wanting to stop my own folding, packing,
taping shut of intimate things. Only when I
paused to sip your favorite tea, caught
the scent of you in the bedroom, did I sense
you watching, reminding me how creases
fold themselves into familiar patterns,
how garments must be draped
as if they're to be worn again, even
if by someone else. No boxes can hold
all these notions, no container sturdy enough
to carry absence. Cardboard and plastic
seem too inconsequential to care
for all that adorned you. As I dim the lights,
sit near you on the loveseat, I notice
the standing mirror has turned slightly
toward me, and in the closet,
one carton re-opened.

*To be human among people and to remain one forever,
no matter what the circumstances, not to grow despondent
and not to lose heart—that's what life is about, that's its task.*
—Fyodor Dostoevsky

# About the Author

Alan Perry is a poet and editor. His debut chapbook, *Clerk of the Dead,* was a finalist in the Cathy Smith Bowers Poetry Competition, and was released by Main Street Rag Publishing (2020). His poems have appeared in *Tahoma Literary Review, Valparaiso Poetry Review, Third Wednesday, San Pedro River Review, ONE ART, Gyroscope Review, Stone Circle Review,* and elsewhere. Founder and Co-Managing Editor of *RockPaperPoem,* a Senior Poetry Editor for *Typehouse Magazine,* and a Best of the Net nominee, Alan lives with his wife in suburban Minneapolis, MN and Tucson, AZ.

More at:
AlanPerryPoetry.com

www.ingramcontent.com/pod-product-compliance
Lightning Source LLC
Chambersburg PA
CBHW070942160426
43193CB00011B/1779